Canyon Echoes
and other poems

HENRY H. GRAY

authorHOUSE

AuthorHouse™
1663 Liberty Drive
Bloomington, IN 47403
www.authorhouse.com
Phone: 833-262-8899

© 2023 Henry H. Gray. All rights reserved.

No part of this book may be reproduced, stored in a retrieval system, or transmitted by any means without the written permission of the author.

Published by AuthorHouse 01/31/2023

ISBN: 978-1-7283-7716-2 (sc)
ISBN: 978-1-7283-7714-8 (hc)
ISBN: 978-1-7283-7715-5 (e)

Library of Congress Control Number: 2023900630

Print information available on the last page.

Any people depicted in stock imagery provided by Getty Images are models, and such images are being used for illustrative purposes only.
Certain stock imagery © Getty Images.

Interior and back cover photos by Henry H. Gray and family.

This book is printed on acid-free paper.

Because of the dynamic nature of the Internet, any web addresses or links contained in this book may have changed since publication and may no longer be valid. The views expressed in this work are solely those of the author and do not necessarily reflect the views of the publisher, and the publisher hereby disclaims any responsibility for them.

Foreword

This book's for browsing.
Dog-ear the page you might wish to read again,
and browse on.

A scattering of poems herein are from my earlier
book, *A Few Poems for Alice* (Author House, 2015)
and are reprinted here with permission.

I dedicate this little volume to the memory
of my late wife, Alice, who encouraged my writing.

The layout and cover for this book
were designed by Finn Boulding.

Canyon Echoes

They lived here many years ago,
Men, women, children of another race.
For generations they wrought a living
From this dry, forbidding place.

They lived here, raised their families,
But wrote no words to mark their passing.
Houses now are silent, voices quelled,
Fields barren, temples unattended.

What brought them here, what unknown forces,
What war, plague, famine drove them here,
Then led them on to other unknown places,
Leaving whispering winds to tell their stories –

The Game

Each day I play the game,
the Game of Life.
One major rule there is:
I play the hand I'm dealt
however difficult that may be.
Oh, now and then
I may request another card
and trade in one I've held since birth.
But no matter how skillfully I play,
in the end the house will win.

Oak Leaves

Oak leaves –
Thousands from the same tree,
Each one unique
But each one guided
By the same set of instructions
Printed in their genes.

Infinite variety in similarity –
Just like people.

The tiny
    golden leaf
has left
    its twig
        and
           is slowly
  finding its way
to the
    ground –
      it sashays
          this way
    and that
  until finally
      it gracefully
          settles
        on the ground – for now

The Bright Trail

The snail
Crept carefully across the spider's web
And left suspended a film of silver,
A floating fragment
Of the sky.

Ambition

Once I wrote a poem
That reached higher, higher, higher,
As I tried to touch the stars.
But alas, my poem crumbled
And fell into a pile of words around my feet.
Here a word glimmered,
There a line protruded from the pile.
What shall I do with this wreckage?
I bent, and stacked the pieces neatly,
Hoping someday to begin anew,
When I shall stay closer to that
Which I know.

Crystal Clarity

In class of long ago I studied crystal forms,
Beginning, so I thought, with least complex,
A pyramid, it seemed, with just three faces.
It did not yield to my analysis, and
Teacher, noting my confusion,
Snatched the model from my hand.
"That's tougher than it seems," she said,
And handed me another one. From that
I went on to conquer icositetrahedrons
And other forms too complex to mention.

Life's Paths

There is a divinity that shapes our ends,
Rough-hew them how we will –
So saith the bard. He's wrong!
The milieu into which we're born
Lays out a network of paths
From which we choose
This way or that, fine-tuning only
Our walk through life.

Frost

I know why
The frost on my window pane,
In the skim of ice on my birdbath,
On the leaves of my shrubbery,
Forms delicate, beautiful crystals.

This is because
The ions of hydrogen and oxygen
That make up the crystals
Are of such size that they must
Fit together in a definite hexagonal pattern.

But the knowledge
Of this process does not in the least
Diminish my admiration of its effect,
Of its beauty, of its variety –
And I marvel at it each time that it appears.

Fine Art

My window pane is streaked by rain
        that does not blur, but softens
all the edges of the features in my view.
        No chiaroscuro, no trompe l'oeil,
a scene no artist could portray –
        but it will be gone in minutes,
with a stronger dash of rain.

Kansas Prairie

Kansas, Flint Hills, tallgrass prairie –
vast grasslands, hip deep or deeper,
once tended by frequent wildfires set,
if not by lightning, then by native peoples
to drive the buffalo, thus keeping
shrubs and trees at bay. Today the fires
are checked, so shrubs and trees
invade the draws where now they capture
scanty moisture. But yet,
vast skylines, sunsets, prairie thunderstorms,
many so far away that they are seen, not heard.
The constant wind caresses the grasses
into waves that rival the ocean's.
These prairies are not
to be passed by easily.
They are not empty –
They are brimming
with life.

St. Joseph Beach

We'd walked a bit along the beach – again –
Then took the steps that led us
Up and over the dune
That bordered the beach.
At the top a small enclosure
Offered shelter from the constant wind,
And here my lady sat to rest.
I said I'd bring the car a little closer
And turning, watched as she took
A last long look
At the sea –

Redtail Hawk

From our vantage point, the valley below,
deepened and widened by ancient tongues of ice,
was in the foreground of our panoramic view.

Deep below us in the valley we saw a bird,
tiny in the distance, describing spirals,
rising higher, higher, higher,

as with each loop it came
closer, closer, closer,
to our point of view.

Now we could see it was a Redtail Hawk,
so close it seemed we could almost touch it.
It twitched its primary feathers

as it adjusted its attitude,
still rising, rising, rising,
until far above us, again it became tiny.

Then with another adjustment we couldn't see
it sharply set off on a southwest tangent
to new lands, new vistas, new hunting sites –

January

Two-headed Janus —
Why does he mark the beginning of the year?
Like Janus, we look behind, make resolutions,
then look ahead,
But Janus mans the gate, the portal
Through which we walk
To parts unknown.

Fragments of a Life

We'd walked a mile along the beach.
    She walked on, but now I turn, retrace
My steps and notice — here footprints stay,
    There they're gone, obliterated, where
Tongues of swash raced higher up the beach.

And so it is with memory —
    Some remains, some's gone.
Eventually the tide comes in and then
    All memory will be erased.

Your Universe

Don't hurry through life –

Look – look at all around you
but also see, see everything around you,
the world, the sky, the universe.

Listen – listen to all around you
but also hear, hear everything around you,
the world, the sky, the universe.

Sense it all, *engage* it all,
from the soil at your feet to the farthest galaxy –
it's your world, your sky, your universe!

Connections

If, as I have read,
The flight of a butterfly in the Philippines
May set off a tornado in Kansas,
    It is because everything is connected to everything else.

If the teeter goes up when the totter goes down,
If my hip bone connects to my leg bone,
If I can see a distant galaxy,
    It is because everything is connected to everything else.

If we share most of our genes with a chimpanzee,
If atoms link firmly to create delicate crystals,
If ecologists tell me that I cannot do just one thing,
    It is because everything is connected to everything else.

If my great uncle is your seventh cousin,
If six degrees of separation connect me to you
Or to anyone else in the world,
    It is because everyone is connected to everyone else.

So if everything is connected to everything else
And everyone is connected to everyone else,
That means that everything and everyone
    Must be parts of a universe –

Take care of it!

One of mankind's
    best ideas,
        B
        r
        i
        d
        g
        e
        s
    Are meant
to bring people together.

The Barber Shop, 1935

I am old enough now
That I can have my hair cut
In a real barber shop –
Not in the beauty parlor on the third floor
Of the big department store.

So today I emerge from the shop
Into the din of the street corner to the shout
Of the news butcher: "Read all about it!
"Will Rogers and Wiley Post killed –
"Plane crash in Alaska!"

Promptly I shift into denial. Can't be,
Mustn't be, I insist. I look for help
From the news butcher, from the fat cop
Who also occupies this corner,
But they offer none.

Even sight and smell
Of doughnuts frying in the kettle
In the shop across the way, usually fascinating
As they flip themselves over, but this
Cannot distract me today – no.

I walk slowly down the street.
Tears streaming, I ignore the
Steamship model in the travel agent's window.
I'd always stopped to admire it,
But not today – no.

Can't be, mustn't be – no.
On to grandma's house for help.

First Love?

We briefly met at Freshman mixer.
One or two dances, switched partners,
And she was gone.
Only then I realized
I had not learned her name.
It took me weeks to find her again.

We then went to plays, concerts, dances,
And enjoyed deep discussions
On the long return commute.
I think I was in love with her
But did not know how to tell her
Or how to ask her feelings.

But there was a war on,
And when she turned eighteen
She felt needed at her home across the sea –
Yet in departing she left room
For another.

We Are Such Stuff

We are such stuff as everything is made of,
Of elements, once ninety-two, now more,
All mutable, interchanging as the years march on.
Thus we all are parts of life, of earth, of stars,
Offspring of the Big Bang –

The New Chapter

I had thought
That I had come to the final lines
Of my poetry. But then
I read a book
That opened a whole new chapter
In my mind.
Now I need to find
If I can express
The essence of that book,
Its germinal idea,
In a few lines
Of poetry –

Beginnings?

Leeuwenhoek, with his tiny microscopes,
discovered microscopic beings,
some of which were bacteria.

Linnaeus then organized all life forms —
there are plants and there are animals,
but what are bacteria, plants or animals?

Darwin knew nothing of bacteria
and thus could not connect them
into his trees of life.

But there are organisms that
are not even bacteria —
their RNAs are not up to snuff!

What are these too simple things,
Extremophiles, that may form the base
of the tangled tree of life —

Thermophiles, acidophiles, methanogens,
all inhabit impossible places —
archaea, are they beginnings of life?

Agony or Ecstasy

A line lies hotly on my brow
At four A.M. I leap from bed
And scribble down a line or two,
Then back to bed, but no!
I cannot rest, another line,
Another leap, and so it goes.
The hours pass close. So are these lines
Worth moments of sweet slumber lost?
Morning, if ever it comes, may tell.

Walking

We walked a long way together,
Through forests of pine and spruce,
Of oak and hickory,
Over prairie and tundra,
Endless beaches, desert sand,
And miles of mountain rock
Strewn with alpine flowers
That struggle for life in tiny crevices.
We watched clouds, sunsets,
Rainbows, moon and stars,
And listened to the birds,
Always finding interest
In all that was around us.

Those walks are over now. I walk alone.
My walks are shorter and less frequent,
But if I look, there are clouds, stars, sunsets,
And the birds still sing —

Pacific K4s

A monster.
Great heaving, hulking, hissing mass,
Wheels and rods below, surmounted by a
Huge steel cylinder, full of fire and water,
That carries all the bells and whistles.
Once she streaked across the countryside
Sixty, seventy, eighty miles an hour
Followed by a string of coaches, Pullmans
And most important, a luxurious dining car.
"This is the engine that pulls the train
Across the country and back again,"
As my old nursery rhyme read.

Today she is quiet – brilliantly polished, clean,
But dead, cold, on exhibit with her sisters
So that we may wonder at
How magnificent a monster
She once was.

Paoli Local

Bala-Cynwyd, Merion, Narberth, Ardmore,
Haverford, Bryn Mawr, Villanova, Berwyn –
Singing names in several languages.
Then Paoli, where passengers once changed
For trains traveling farther westward,
As many times I did.

The old cars now are gone
And high-speed SEPTA trains
Serve the Main Line and farther –
But the singing names remain.

Six Epigrams

Look closely –
There's a whole world
In a glistering dewdrop.

    Party line –
    Lonesome wire
    Connecting neighbors.

        Shadows –
        Flickering imitations of life
        Come and go.

Clouds –
Ever-changing
Magical kingdoms.

It's pouring –
But when clouds unload,
Skies brighten.

Darning needle –
It hovers, it flits, it zooms,
It's gone!

Sagebrush

Once I spent an afternoon
    alone on a sagebrush flat.
My partner, far away,
    signaled me to sight in
this point or that. Meanwhile
    I had time to sense
the details of my surroundings.
    I always liked the odor
of the sagebrush, and I watched
    the ants that busily
brought up grains of sand,
    among which were tiny
striated cubes of pyrite. Coyotes
    from their burrows, unseen,
sang arias, duets, dirges,
    each one sadder than the last.
I can now recall the sights, the sounds –
    but not the aroma of the sagebrush,
freshened by a morning shower.

Sand

Millions and millions of grains on the beach,
And each one would have its own story to tell –
If only I could hear.

Each one's unique in process and source.
This one is garnet and this one is quartz,
This has inclusions and this one does not,
This one is rounded and this one is not.
Their stories extend over millions of years,
Of limitless travels with many long rests
Until at last they now lie in my hand –
If only I could hear.

Dancing Shadows

Shadows dancing on the leaves,
Fluttering, flittering, fleeting –
A butterfly is feeding.

Foggy Morning

Shafts of sunlight find their way
    Through openings between the leaves
And in their shining paths
    They seem to be diverging –
Though I know they're really parallel.

Butterfly

The lepidopterist
Studies the butterfly
From a strictly scientific point of view –
Size, colors, habits, geographic distribution,
And many other properties
But in so doing he may miss
Its essential beauty.

Moonrise

I have sometimes watched the full moon slowly rise
From first glimmer, minute by minute by minute
Until at last the orb, looking a bit larger than usual,
Gradually lifts free from the far horizon.

And during these minutes, waiting, I reflect
Upon the times when men of long ago
Also watched the moonrise, noting the phases,
The cycles, the tides, the comings and goings,

And knowing nothing of the motions of Earth and Moon
They wondered at the patterns of these happenings.
Today we know the reasons, the movements of these bodies,
But should we not also retain a sense of wonder?

The Cape

The waves still break on the beach where last I heard them,
    Long ago.
The light still glows on the headland where last I saw it,
    Long ago.
I can recall them, hear them, see them from that time,
    Long ago.
Memories will fade, the light will go out,
    But the waves will break on that beach as they did
        Long ago.

Just Listen!

I ran across a list of questions
For analyzing poetry.
What tone, what symbols, words,
What image does the poet project,
What meter, rhyme, whatever!

I reject this system of analysis,
These picky questions!
Would you dissect a nightingale
To find the motif of his song?
Just listen!

Wood Thrush

The notes of a wood thrush,
Liquid silver in the silent woods,
Become diamonds
In the rain.

Each morning
    It's a whole new world –
Open your heart
    And engage it!

The wintry sunset
builds stained glass windows
as it filters between
bare branches

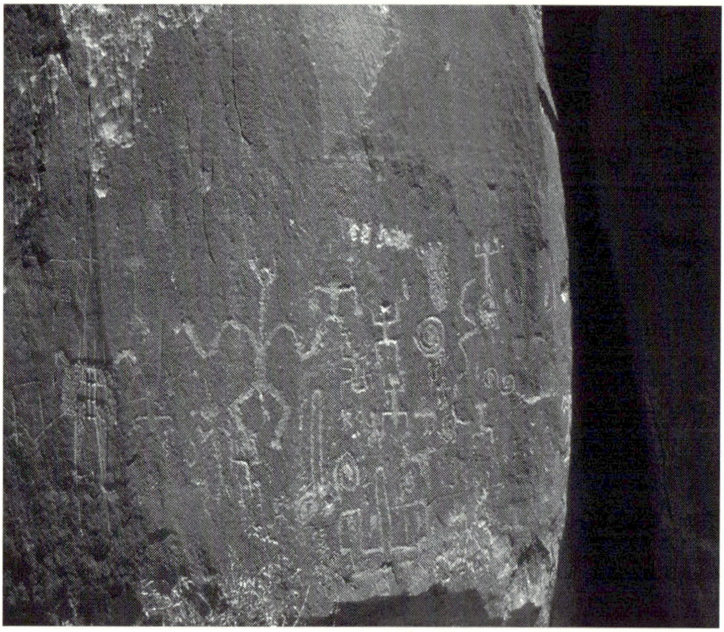

The Storied Rock

They speak to me,
These mystic beings
And cryptic symbols
Pecked into otherwise silent rock.
They speak to me through silences
Of centuries, of eons,
They speak unto eternities,
Expressing thoughts of those
Who've gone before,
Whether I understand them
Or not.

The Presence

Once, exploring an ancient ruin,
I turned over a fragment of pottery,
A shard, and on the other side
Quite clearly shown were
Prints of the potter's finger,
Whorls, neatly aligned in rows
Like scales of a fish.
The hair on the back of my neck
Rose, as I strongly felt
The presence of that person,
Separated from me by a thousand years.

After but a moment of reflection
I carefully replaced the piece
So that another, perhaps
A thousand years hence,
May make the same connection.

Now and Then

As my past gets long and longer
Why do events I know are recent
Fade fast and faster away?

Yesterday seems long ago
And last week seems as distant
As my childhood days.

Distance, direction, volume,
Can be measured in so many ways
But I see only two aspects of time –
Now and then.

This Thing Called Love

What is this thing called love?
It has neither form nor dimension,
No width, no length, no height, no volume.
The heart can hold an infinite amount of it
Where it can be shared with
Friends, relations – and yet
It can also embrace the entire World.
I say it can, but more's the point,
It must displace hate.

You Never Know

You never know
When is the last time,
The last time you see someone you love,
The last time you eat your favorite meal,
The last time you see a favorite scene
Or the ocean or the mountains.

You never know
Because you know only what is past,
Not what the future brings, and so
You must savor each moment, if you can,
As though it is your last, because
You never know.

A Fragment

What feeble flames are we who rail against the darkness,
The black unknown that wraps around us all,
We know not what's ahead, forget what's behind us,
As memory dims and shrouds us like a pall.

This dark stanza
now seeks a purpose.

And All Our Yesterdays

Where have all our yesterdays gone,
    So soon, so soon, so soon,
Our childhood, youthful yesterdays,
    Where have they gone?
And how did we find each other,
    To join together for so many years,
And when did our children leave the nest,
    So soon, so soon, so soon,
Yes, where have all those yesterdays gone –
    Where are they now, our yesterdays?

Time, the Tyrant

Time and tide wait for no man
Is an adage so ancient
That Bartlett's doesn't list it –
But it goes back to Chaucer,
If not deeper.

You may set the clock back,
But that's an artifice
Because time moves one way only.
The tick of my clock, the beat of my heart,
Mark small bits of time,
Each of them gone, never to return.

The nick of time may be too close,
Because a miss is as good as a mile.
If you miss the kickoff,
You may watch the rest of the game,
But if the bus left just a minute ago,
The station's empty.

There are times when
Time hangs heavy on my mind,
But time will tell.
The time will come when it
Will march on without me,
And I won't notice.

My Seventh Age

My seventh age is still ahead,
    My first now far behind.
These both are blank, but all the rest,
    Ages to Shakespeare, come to mind
As strands of life that plait into
    A braid as do these lines of mine.
Schoolboy, lover, scholar, and all the rest
    Are threads with roots, but yet no ends.
These all remain as I approach
    My final stage, with eyes, ears
And more that all need help, with slippers
    (But not pantaloons!), a patriarch
Perhaps, as I await my seventh age,
    The last.

The Wayward Word –

Why do words, names, slip from my mind, get lost,
    Only to return when not needed?
Are there black holes somewhere in my brain?
    There seemingly are no leaks
As words, names from a distant past can
    Suddenly erupt, demand attention,
Though as a rule by now they're useless.
    But when I need a word today, right now,
It often seems to be among the missing.

The Right Word

Often I want the just right word,
    The lightning, not the bug,
The flash, not the fizzle,
    The wow, not the wimp –
But I must await that blinding strike
    When suddenly I realize, *that's it!*

On the Pond

    Breezes gently kiss the water,
        Sending skifts of wavelets
            This way and that –

A Vignette

Frost on the dry oak leaf –
A delicate fringe of tiny crystals
Like fine needlework,
But it will vanish
With the sun.

A Winter's Tale

It's cold. The hole in the soil,
No bigger than my little finger,
Is rimmed with small spears of frost.

Somewhere below a tiny body breathes,
And with each exhalation warm moisture flows
To the mouth of its abode and crystallizes there.

The fox knows all this, but also knows that
The creature below is far too small
To be worth digging from the frozen ground.

Nevermore

Once we spent a night
    at an empty campground
in an empty state.
    In the silence, silence, silence,
we watched the shadows lengthen
    until the stars came out.

Infrequent cars took many minutes
    to pass from sight
on the highway far away.
    In the silence, silence, silence,
only distant headlamps
    proclaimed their passing.

A raven had welcomed us
    to his campground. We named
him "Nevermore," and it seems
    that was the right thing to do,
because it was here that we, unknowingly,
    enjoyed our final campfire.

Brief Encounter

I danced with her but once.
It must have been set up, because
I was too bashful to have asked.
We'd never met before –
I never saw her again –
And that was more than eighty years ago,
So tell me, please, why does her name
Leap from my deepest memories now?

The Survivor

The small white oak had given up
Its quest for life on rocky ledge
In our small ravine.
I felled it, cut it into lengths
And doing so I noticed
Close-packed growth rings,
Like grooves on a music disc.

    So I polished one cut
    And set about counting
    The annual rings. In a tree
    Scarce eight inches
    In diameter, I counted
    One hundred thirty of them!

This tree was a mere sprout
When our land was transferred
To its first private owner
Who promptly harvested his forest.
Passed over, the twig grew rapidly
Some twenty years, then slowed
As better nourished trees shaded it
And the rings became thin.

> But then, a hundred years later,
> Thick rings again recorded rapid growth.
> Larger trees had again been harvested
> Allowing this small one to grow again.
> But, history repeating, new forest cover,
> Trees more favorably sited shaded it,
> Thin rings again recorded slow, slow growth,
> Until the day it gave up,
> Waiting for my saw.

Oak Leaf

Red oak leaf, *Quercus rubra,*
Sharply pointed lobes,
Seven in all.
Burnished dark brown
Like old leather,
It has served its purpose
And now lies forgotten
On the forest floor,
But not unobserved –
It's November.

The Not-so-lost Muse

My muse had fled to other parts.
She'd left no forwarding address.
But then I saw a shaft of sunlight
That brightly fell upon a fallen leaf.
Aha! I thought, now there's a tale
That I can cast as poetry!
I'm glad my muse has suddenly
Found her way home.

A Pleasant Spot for Lunch

Somewhere in Idaho,
Seeking a lunch spot, I found
A slight rise from which
I could see the beaver meadows,
The plain beyond, and mountains
That defined my horizon.
But as I chose my place to sit
I saw that someone
Had been here before me,
For surrounding my site
Was a debitage
Of obsidian flakes –

Aspen in the Fall

Sparkling shafts of sunlight fall
On amber leaves and on
The ground beneath, and where
A ray of sunlight strikes a fallen leaf
It's doubly bright.

The List

The box is hard to open – it's been about a year –
But there they are, all lined up A through Z,
Of course no X's, Z's, surprisingly, perhaps, no F's.
There's Ken, old college friend, not heard from
Since ninety-two. And Sam and Jean,
Where are they now? My cousins send religious cards –
No messages, just signatures. Our list
Built up as years went by – one year we sent
Two hundred cards! But that was long ago.
The list gets shorter, as now the world
Consists of people that I do not know.

The Older I Get

The older I get the more it seems that
I'm easily addled
Readily rattled
Frequently flustered
Can't cut the mustard
Diverted confounded
Distracted dumbfounded
Deluded confused
Bewildered bemused
Often forgetful
Also neglectful
Can't keep my head on
Easily led on –
No wonder I cannot get anything done!

My View

The world explodes into a symphony of green,
    A subtle tint creeps up the forest slope
That then explodes into a brash viridian –
    This ever-changing view outside my window.

Hot, glowing colors follow. Flames of saffron,
    Orange, crimson, sulfur spread the ground
That yields its bounty with abandon. This is
    The scene that now delights my window.

And now a russet, gold and umber scarf
    Bedecks the slopes that lie across the way.
Dry leaves sweep noisily across my porch –
    Another change of scene outside my window.

The leaden days that follow may bring snow
    Or frost that rims the relict leaves with crystals.
Is this a cycle, or may there be at last
    An end to all I see outside my window?

Talking Trees

Towering trees, reaching for the sky,
But, more important, connecting underground,
Sharing information, sustenance, through rootlets
That entangle with fungal mycelia in the soil.
This process, little known until recently,
Is important as we learn more –
How better to restore our forests.

***Cypress* –**

Silent sentinels of the swamp,
      Tall beyond belief, yet anchored solidly
In the uncertain ground –

***Sycamore* –**

At the end of my lane stands a sycamore,
      Trunk golden in the rays of setting sun,
Starkly etched against the sullen sky –

Blue-tailed Skink –

Silvery, slithery, silently,
      Its tapered form slides effortlessly
            Between the spears of grass,
                  Scarcely showing its trail –

Dark Thoughts

In the nadir of the night,
      At three or four, when aches and pains
That seem like nothing in the day
      Rob me of sleep, why must my thoughts
Turn dark? I am, therefore I think,
      But why cannot I guide my thoughts
To those of happier days? Why can't I think
      Of shoes or ships or sealing wax
Or any other things not dark – why not?
      Again a line lies heavy on my brow,
But how may I now erase it?

Donora, PA
October 1948

Darkness at midday.
Smoke that means prosperity
Should rise, disperse,
Instead hangs low within the valley.

Air reeks of sulfur,
Soot clouds the sidewalks,
Cars move slowly, headlights on.
How long must this hell continue?

Doctors are busy
Treating illnesses they know not what.
Respiratory failures one by one
Expand the death rate.

On the football field, the big game,
Players scarcely see each other –
It's days before the pall lifts
And life returns to the valley.

This event is one of those that led to
The Environmental Protection Act

The Occasional Poet

Poems don't flow lightly from my hand.
      In fits and starts and nows and thens
They find their way across the page.

Sometimes a word, sometimes a phrase
      Calls forth a line that builds, expands,
And shapes itself into a poem.

Sometimes, instead, words fail.

Things Left Undone

Among those things that don't get done
      Are those that simply weren't begun
And those that were done half-way
      And put off for another day.

The Truth Prevails

There were those who thought Galileo was wrong,
    But the truth shone through.
Barbarians stormed against the gates,
    But the truth shone through.
Vandals burned libraries again and again,
    But the truth shone through.
The truth rises up to be struck down again,
    But in time the truth prevails –

The Wall

There is a wall
that doesn't divide neighbors.

It lies, half buried, between
towering monuments
to two of the greatest men
this republic has ever produced.

Inscribed upon the granite of this wall are
names of thousands of men and women
who gave their lives for this nation
in a land far, far away.

I did not, cannot know any of those
whose names are recorded on this wall,
but they all were known, loved, awaited
by someone, somewhere.

A pair of booties, a book, a rose, a combat boot
lay at the foot of this wall when I saw it.
These surely now are lost. The wall endures
so that our memory must not fade.

The Darkest Hour

I am adrift upon a roiling sea.
My sail, my rudder, compass, all are gone.
The darkling night folds in. My craft –
What is her name? And all my yesterdays,
My yesterdays fade into oblivion. But yet recall,
The darkest hour is just before the dawn.

CONTENTS

Canyon Echoes 1
The Game 3
Oak Leaves 5
The tiny golden leaf 7
The Bright Trail 9
Ambition 11
Crystal Clarity 13
Life's Paths 15
Frost 17
Fine Art 19
Kansas Prairie 21
St. Joseph Beach 23
Redtail Hawk 25
January 27
Fragments of a Life 29
Your Universe 31
Connections 33
Bridges 35
The Barber Shop, 1935 37
First Love? 39
We Are Such Stuff 41
The New Chapter 43
Beginnings? 45
Agony or Ecstasy 47
Walking 49
Pacific K4s 51
Paoli Local 53
Six Epigrams 54
Sagebrush 57
Sand 59
Dancing Shadows 60
Foggy Morning 60
Butterfly 61
Moonrise 63
The Cape 65
Just Listen! 67

Wood Thrush	69
Each morning	70
The wintry sunset	71
The Storied Rock	73
The Presence	75
Now and Then	77
This Thing Called Love	79
You Never Know	81
A Fragment	83
And All Our Yesterdays	85
Time, the Tyrant	87
My Seventh Age	89
The Wayward Word –	90
The Right Word	91
On the Pond	92
A Vignette	93
A Winter's Tale	95
Nevermore	97
Brief Encounter	99
The Survivor	100
Oak Leaf	103
The Not-so-lost Muse	105
A Pleasant Spot for Lunch	107
Aspen in the Fall	109
The List	111
The Older I Get	113
My View	115
Talking Trees	117
Cypress –	118
Sycamore –	118
Blue-tailed Skink –	119
Dark Thoughts	121
Donora, PA October 1948	123
The Occasional Poet	125
Things Left Undone	127
The Truth Prevails	129
The Wall	131
The Darkest Hour	133

also by **Henry H. Gray**

A Few Poems for Alice

available from **AuthorHouse**